Freezer Meals

Quick and Easy Money-Saving Recipes

Jenny Davis

Just to say "thank you" for buying this book, I'd like to give you a gift *absolutely free*

Top Homemade Dip and Spread Recipes

To claim your copy, simply go to:
www.alvobooks.com/diprecipes

Contents

Introduction

The recipes in this book have all been designed to save you time by curtailing the hours you spend cooking. This will give you precious hours back to spend time with your family and friends, or do something else you enjoy. By taking a little time at the start of the week or month to prepare bulk meals, you'll free up your days, and enjoy better health and well-being.

The recipes in this book will help you:

Save time and eliminate stress

Just one day of preparation can yield up to a month's worth of meals! This upfront preparation can also save a month's worth of stress at dinner time, which, as all working parents know, is priceless. Not having to worry about dinner each night just makes life so much easier.

Save money

As for saving money, you do this in three ways. Firstly, buying food in bulk is typically a lot cheaper than buying individual amounts. Secondly, planning your meals in advance and freezing them eliminates waste. Thirdly, you no longer need to order take-out or buy commercial frozen dinners.

Enjoy nutritious meals

Beyond the obvious benefits of saving time and money, preparing and freezing your own homemade meals allows you to make sure your family is eating nutritious foods. You know exactly what is in your food, unlike at restaurants or with prepackaged frozen meals.

Now, with all these advantages, there is no reason to spend hours cooking every night, nor order take-out. By storing food in meal-sized portions, you can get out that evening's meal in the morning, allow it to thaw all day, and then heat it up at dinner time.

Freezer meals offer options that everyone can benefit from, so what are you waiting for?

Let's get started!

Basics for Freezing, Thawing, and Food Safety

Before we get started, there are a few important things to know about freezing and food safety. Don't worry – these points are all very simple and straight-forward.

Freezing Tips

Although you can freeze almost any food and it will be safe, some ingredients do lose some of their quality when frozen. It's best to freeze foods at their prime state of freshness and quality, as they will be in better condition when thawed later. Freezing also keeps the vitamin content, flavor and colors intact.

Avoiding Freezer Burn

One thing to be aware of when freezing meals is freezer burn. You've probably seen frozen food that has grey or brown marks on it – this is freezer burn. While it's not dangerous and has no impact on health, it is unsightly and unappetizing.

In order to prevent freezer burn, you should keep your meals sealed in airtight containers or bags. Great options are Tupperware containers or sealable plastic bags, like Ziploc bags. You want to prevent your food from coming in contact with air, so always aim to remove as much air as possible from the bags or containers.

If you find that you love the freezer meals approach, consider investing in a vacuum sealer. You can pick them up for just $100-$150 and they make sure that all of the air is completely removed, so you're fully protected from freezer burn. Also, vacuum-sealed packs are compact, allowing you to make the most of your freezer space.

Food Safety Prior to Freezing

At temperatures around 0°F (-18°C), the microorganisms that cause food to spoil and cause illness become dormant. However, care needs to be taken during the preparation stages.

Follow these safety tips:

1. Keep raw ingredients chilled in the fridge until you are ready to make your recipe.

2. Keep ingredients at similar temperatures – never add hot sauces to cold meats. Instead, make sure you cool all sauces first, before combining them with other chilled ingredients.

3. Use bags and containers that seal properly and remove as much air as possible.

4. When freezing soups or liquids, remember that they will expand, so leave an inch gap at the top of containers.

5. Prepare, cool, then freeze meals as quickly as possible – do not freeze any foods that have been left out at temperatures above 40°F (5°C – or warmer than your fridge) for more than two hours, in order to avoid food-borne illnesses.

6. Cool food before placing in the freezer (this prevents your freezer heating up, which could jeopardize food

that's already frozen). To cool food, place sealed bags or containers into cold or iced water.

7. Freeze in appropriate serving sizes. For example, if you have a family of four, freeze enough for a family meal.

8. Label food with the name of the dish and the date.

What to Freeze and What Not to Freeze

When it comes to freezer meals, there are a few guidelines about what you should and should not freeze for best results. While nothing will go bad when frozen, some things will lose texture and potentially not reheat very well.

Many people are unsure whether or not they can freeze vegetables. In general, veggies with a low water content freeze quite well, and blanching for 30 seconds in hot water prior to freezing also improves results. Green beans, carrots, squash, peas, and corn are some vegetables that freeze well.

Freezing fruit is a great way of dealing with excess when everything seems to ripen at once! Wash, peel, and cut the fruit and then freeze in handy portions for smoothies. Bananas, berries, peaches, plums, grapes, and mangos are among many fruits that freeze very well.

Here are a few basic guidelines to help you decide what you should and shouldn't freeze:

Do Freeze

1. Meats, poultry, and fish
2. Bread
3. Butter and margarine
4. Cooked beans
5. Flours and nuts (to extend shelf life)
6. Fruit and veggies with low water content
7. Sauces that aren't egg-based
8. Raw pastry
9. Hard, shredded cheeses like Parmesan

Freeze with Caution (may change in texture)

1. Milk, cheese, and yoghurt
2. Herbs

Don't Freeze

1. Select vegetables (lettuce, celery, cucumbers, radishes, and other veggies with a high water content)
2. Melons and other fruit with a high water content
3. Raw and hard-boiled eggs
4. Mayonnaise and other eggy sauces
5. Gelatin

Thawing Tips

The biggest concern with defrosting your frozen meals safely is preventing food-borne illnesses. The bacteria and parasites that cause illnesses cannot multiply in the freezer, but once food reaches temperatures above 40°F (5°C), the bacteria can begin to multiply rapidly. Therefore, use one of these three methods to thaw your frozen meals:

1. Microwave – Use this method only if you are going to cook the meal immediately after heating. This is because the meal can start to cook in the microwave.

2. Thaw in the refrigerator – Plan ahead as most foods will take about a day to thaw in the fridge. This is a good method if you take your meal out of the freezer before going to work in the morning.

3. Thaw in cold water – This method is quick, but you must be careful. Store food in a bag or package that will not leak. You want to protect your meal from bacteria in the air. You also don't want the meal to absorb any water. The water should be refreshed every half hour to keep the meal thawing out continuously.

If you have not thawed your meal at all, you can actually cook it from frozen, but factor in an additional 50% of the original cooking time.

Once you have thawed a meal, avoid re-freezing it. While some foods thawed in the fridge may still be safe to re-freeze, there will be a loss of quality.

Preparation

All the meals in this book can be made individually, or in bulk. Some of them are fully prepared before freezing, while others are raw or partially precooked. What they have in common is that they're all easy to reheat or finish at a later time.

Now all you have to do is plan your preparation schedule. The truth about preparing freezer meals is that the right method depends on your preferences and lifestyle. There is no perfect answer, and it usually takes some testing to find the prep that works best for you. Some people love taking a whole day (often with friends) to prepare meals for the month ahead. Others like working one week at a time. A great option can also be to team up with friends, family, and neighbors and have a frozen meals swap so you can all benefit from each other's work. Of course, there are also people who just want to have a few meals tucked away for a rainy, busy day.

There are many ways these meals can help make life a bit more convenient, so find what is right for you!

Sides

Caramelized Sweet Potatoes with Apples
Serves 4-6

Ingredients:
5 sweet potatoes (cooked, peeled, and cubed)
4 apples (peeled, cored, and sliced)
1/2 cup brown sugar
1/2 teaspoon salt
4 tablespoons butter
1 teaspoon ground nutmeg
1/2 teaspoon ground cinnamon
1/4 cup hot water
2 tablespoons honey
Non-stick cooking spray

Directions:
1. Heat the oven to 350° F (175°Celsius) and grease a casserole dish with non-stick cooking spray.

2. Layer just enough sweet potatoes to cover the bottom of the dish, then top with a layer of sliced apples.

3. Sprinkle a fine layer of sugar, salt, and small pieces of butter.

4. Repeat the steps above and continue layering the ingredients in the casserole dish.

5. On the top layer of apples, sprinkle the remaining brown sugar and butter pieces.

6. Top with nutmeg and cinnamon.

7. Mix the hot water and honey together in a saucepan over low heat. Pour the mix over the top layer.

8. Bake for about 30 minutes or until the apples are tender and the top of the bake is golden.

Freeze it: Allow the contents to cool completely. Transfer to a freezer bag or storage container of your choice. Make sure you label it with the date and dish name.

Reheat it: Thaw the contents in the refrigerator. Microwave in portions or reheat in the oven at 350°F (175°C) for about 10 minutes.

Nutrition Facts per Serving:
Calories: 237
Fat: 8 grams
Sodium: 236 mg
Sugar: 37 grams
Protein: 2 grams

Cheesy Green Beans
Serves 4

Ingredients:
1 tablespoon vegetable oil
1 medium onion (diced)
3 tablespoons cornstarch
1 cup milk
1 cup mozzarella cheese (shredded)
1 teaspoon salt
18 ounces green beans (trimmed)
2 cups bread crumbs (seasoned)
Non-stick cooking spray

Directions:
1. Heat the oven to 325° F (160°C) and prepare a 9" x 13" casserole dish with non-stick spray.

2. Heat a medium-sized saucepan over medium heat and sauté the diced onion in the oil until it becomes soft.

3. Mix the cornstarch and salt with the milk, then add it to the pan.

4. Stir the mixture and continue to cook it until it thickens.

5. Stir in the cheese.

6. Add the green beans to the casserole dish and pour the sauce on top, then sprinkle over the bread crumbs.

7. Bake for 30-40 minutes.

Freeze it: Allow the contents to cool after baking. Transfer them to a plastic, sealable freezer bag or storage container of your choice. Make sure you label with the date and dish name.

Reheat it: Thaw the frozen beans and cheese in the refrigerator. Reheat in the oven at 325°F (160°C) for about 15 minutes. Alternatively, heat in the microwave for 2-3 minutes per serve.

Nutrition Facts per Serving:
Calories: 243
Fat: 7.5 grams
Sodium: 984 mg
Sugar: 10 grams
Protein: 12.5 grams

Twice-Baked Potatoes

Serves 12 (1 potato each)

Ingredients:

Around 5 pounds baking potatoes, or 1 medium potato per person
1/2 cup melted butter
1 cup milk
2 teaspoons salt
1 teaspoon ground pepper
4 ounces sharp cheddar cheese

Directions:

1. Heat the oven to 350°F (175°C) and prepare a baking sheet.

2. Place the whole potatoes on the baking sheet and bake them for around an hour, or until cooked through.

3. Combine the melted butter, salt, and pepper in a small mixing bowl.

4. Cut the potatoes in half and scoop out the insides, leaving the skins intact.

5. Mix the potato that you removed with the butter and beat until smooth. Add the milk in gradually to reach a creamy consistency.

6. Fill each potato skin with the potato mixture.

7. Sprinkle with cheese.

Freeze it: Place the finished potatoes on the baking sheet, cover with plastic wrap, and freeze for 3 hours. When completely frozen, remove the wrap and transfer the potatoes to a freezer bag or storage container of your choice.

Reheat it: Heat the oven to 350°F (175°C). Place the potatoes on a baking sheet, loosely covered in foil. Bake for 45 minutes, then an additional 5 minutes uncovered. For faster preparation, microwave each for about 10 minutes before baking. They can be reheated in the microwave from frozen, although the skins are crispier when reheated in the oven.

Nutrition Facts per Serving:
Calories: 286
Fat: 11 grams
Sodium: 583 mg
Sugar: 2 grams
Protein: 8 grams

Soups

Chicken and Artichoke Soup with Basil
Serves 4-6

Ingredients:
2 tablespoons olive oil
1 1/3 cups celery (diced)
1 cup onion (diced)
1 clove garlic (minced)
1/2 teaspoon salt
1/2 teaspoon black pepper (freshly ground)
4 cups chicken broth
1 cup artichoke hearts
1 cup fresh spinach
Handful fresh basil (chopped)
2 cups chicken (cooked and shredded)

Directions:
1. Add the olive oil to a large skillet over medium heat and sauté the onion for about 4 to 5 minutes, or until soft.

2. Once the onions have softened, add in the diced celery and sauté for another 5 minutes, then add the garlic and sauté for further minute.

3. Next, add in the chicken broth and artichokes. Bring it to a boil. Then cover, lower the heat to medium-low, and simmer for about 10 minutes.

4. After that time, use an immersion blender to blend the soup, or you can puree small batches in a food processor.

5. Once blended well, season with the salt and black pepper.

6. Cool the soup, then stir in the shredded chicken, basil, and fresh spinach.

Freeze it: Transfer to the freezer bag or container of your choice. Make sure you label it with the date and dish name.

Reheat it: Thaw the frozen soup in the refrigerator or by running warm water over the bag. Reheat in a stock pot on the stovetop over low heat until warm, or use your microwave.

Nutrition Facts per Serving:
Calories: 244
Fat: 9.8 grams
Sodium: 834 mg
Sugar: 3.1 grams
Protein: 26.3 grams

Pearl Barley and Tomato Soup

Serves 4-6

Ingredients:

1 cup yellow onion (chopped)
1 cup celery stalks (chopped)
1 cup carrots (chopped)
2 cloves garlic (minced)
2 tablespoons vegetable oil
1 bay leaf
16-ounce can tomatoes (diced with juice, around 2 cups)
4 cups broth (vegetable or chicken)
1/4 cup pearl barley (uncooked)
Black pepper to taste
Garnish with fresh parsley when serving

Directions:

1. Heat a large saucepan over medium-high heat and add in the onions, carrots, and celery. Sauté for about 5 to 10 minutes or until the onions and celery soften. Then add the garlic and sauté for a further minute.

2. Add in the bay leaf, tomatoes, broth, and barley.

3. Stir while bringing the soup to a boil. Once it reaches a boil, lower the heat and simmer for 40 minutes, or until the barley becomes tender.

4. Remove the bay leaf and add black pepper to taste.

Freeze it: Allow the soup to cool and then transfer it to the freezer bag or container of your choice. Make sure you label it with the date and dish name.

Reheat it: Thaw the frozen soup in the refrigerator or by running warm water over the bag. Reheat in a stock pot on the stovetop over low heat until warm. When serving, sprinkle fresh parsley on top.

Nutrition Facts per Serving:
Calories: 129
Fat: 5.5 grams
Sodium: 455 mg
Sugar: 2 grams
Protein: 4.6 grams

ccoli and Potato Soup

1/4 cup flour
2 cups potatoes (peeled and chopped)
1/2 head broccoli (broken into florets)
1/4 cup celery (diced)
3 cups broth (vegetable or chicken)
2 tablespoons butter
1 cup cheddar cheese (shredded)
1 cup milk
1/2 teaspoon paprika
Salt and freshly-ground black pepper to taste

Directions:

1. Meanwhile, you can melt the butter in a large saucepan over medium heat. Then add in the onions and celery. Sauté until they soften.

2. Once they are soft, add the flour and allow it to brown slightly. Make sure you stir continuously so it doesn't burn.

3. When browned, slowly add in the broth, stirring continuously to ensure no limps form.

4. Once the flour and broth have been combined, add the chopped potatoes, paprika, and milk. Bring to the boil.

5. Lower the heat down so the soup is just simmering, place the lid on and simmer for 15-20 minutes. You want the potatoes to easily break apart with a fork.

6. Once the potatoes have softened, remove the lid and add in the broccoli. Let it cook for a further 3-5 minutes, or until the broccoli is cooked but still has some bite.

7. Remove from the heat and stir the cheese through until it has melted completely. Season the soup to taste. You can choose to leave the soup chunky, or blend it for a smooth soup.

Freeze it: Allow the soup to cool and then transfer it to the freezer bag or container of your choice. Make sure you label it with the date and dish name.

Reheat it: Thaw the frozen soup in the refrigerator or by running warm water over the bag. Reheat in a stock pot on the stovetop over low heat until warm. If you prefer, reheat in your microwave.

Nutrition Facts per Serving:
Calories: 264
Fat: 13 grams
Sodium: 534 mg
Sugar: 2 grams
Protein: 12 grams

Hearty Beef and Vegetable Soup
Serves 8-10

Ingredients:
1 pound ground beef
1 cup onions (diced)
2 cloves garlic (minced)
4 tablespoons olive oil
6 cups beef broth
2 cups celery (roughly chopped)
2 cups carrots (roughly chopped)
2 cups tomatoes (diced)
2 cups skinned sweet potatoes (diced)
1 teaspoon rosemary (dried or fresh)
1 bay leaf
Salt to taste
Pepper to taste
Garnish with fresh parsley when serving

Directions:
1. Heat the olive oil in a large stockpot over medium heat, then add in the diced onions. Sauté them for about 5 minutes, or until soft.

2. Next, add the ground beef to the onions. Cook the beef until completely browned. Drain the fat if needed.

3. Add the garlic and sauté for a further minute.

4. Next, add the broth, tomatoes, celery, sweet potatoes, carrots, and seasonings. Lower the heat, cover, and cook for about 40 minutes. All the veggies should be tender.

5. Remove the bay leaf before freezing.

Freeze it: Allow the soup to cool and then transfer it to the freezer bag or container of your choice. Make sure you label it with the date and dish name.

Reheat it: Thaw the frozen soup in the refrigerator or by running warm water over the bag. Reheat in a stock pot on the stovetop over low heat until warm, or reheat in the microwave. When serving, add salt and pepper to taste, and sprinkle fresh parsley on top.

Nutrition Facts per Serving:
Calories: 396
Fat: 8.6 grams
Sodium: 782 mg
Sugar: 8.8 grams
Protein: 41.4 grams

Butternut Squash Soup

Serves 6-8

Ingredients:
3 tablespoons olive oil
1 large onion (diced)
2 cloves garlic (minced)
4 cups broth (chicken or vegetable)
3 cups tomatoes (diced)
5 cups butternut squash (diced)
1 teaspoon smoked paprika
1 teaspoon thyme (fresh or dried)
Salt and pepper to taste

Directions:
1. Heat the olive oil in a large saucepan over medium-high heat and sauté the onions until soft. Then add the garlic and paprika and sauté for a further 30 seconds.

2. Then add in the broth, diced tomatoes, butternut squash, and thyme. Bring it to a boil.

3. Lower the heat so the soup is simmering. Cover and cook for 30 to 45 minutes or until the squash breaks apart easily.

4. Use an immersion blender to blend the soup, or you can puree small batches in a food processor. If the soup is too thick for your liking, you can add a little water at this stage to dilute it.

5. Adjust the seasoning to taste.

Freeze it: Allow the soup to cool and then transfer it to the freezer bag or container of your choice. Make sure you label it with the date and dish name.

Reheat it: Thaw the frozen soup in the refrigerator or by running warm water over the bag. Reheat in a stock pot on the stovetop over low heat until warm, or in the microwave.

Nutrition Facts per Serving:
Calories: 296
Fat: 2.6 grams
Sodium: 782 mg
Sugar: 8.8 grams
Protein: 4.4 grams

Sausage and Kale Soup
Serves 4

Ingredients:
4 pork sausages
1 cup mushrooms (sliced)
2 cups potatoes (diced)
2 cups kale (chopped)
1/2 cup onion (chopped)
2 tablespoons olive oil
4 cups broth (vegetable or chicken)
2 cloves garlic (minced)
1 teaspoon dried oregano
1/2 teaspoon paprika

Directions:
1. Heat 1 tablespoon olive oil in a large stock pot over medium heat and cook the sausages. Once cooked, remove the sausages, slice them, and reserve.

2. Heat the remaining olive oil in the pot and add in the onion and mushrooms, sauté for 6 to 8 minutes, or until softened.

3. Next, add the garlic and paprika and sauté for a further minute.

4. Then pour the broth into the pot, add the sliced sausage, potatoes, and oregano, and simmer for about 30 minutes, or until the potatoes have broken down.

5. Lastly, add in the kale and cook for about 2 to 5 minutes, until the kale is almost fully wilted. Adjust the seasoning to taste.

Freeze it: Allow the soup to cool and then transfer it to the freezer bag or container of your choice. Make sure you label it with the date and dish name.

Reheat it: Thaw the frozen soup in the refrigerator or by running warm water over the bag. Reheat in a stock pot on the stovetop over low heat until warm, or reheat in the microwave.

Nutrition Facts per Serving:
Calories: 353.8
Fat: 25.3 grams
Sodium: 977.5 mg
Sugar: 2.1 grams
Protein: 22.7 grams

Chicken

Paleo Green Bean and Parsnip Casserole with Chicken
Serves 8

Ingredients:
1 pound parsnips (sliced)
2 pounds green beans (trim ends)
2 tablespoons olive oil
1 1/2 cups onion (sliced)
3 cloves garlic (minced)
2 1/4 cups mushrooms (roughly chopped)
2 teaspoons pepper
2 teaspoons salt
1/4 cup sliced shallots
1 cup chicken stock
3 pounds chicken thighs (skinless and boneless, then cut into bite-size pieces)
Handful chopped nuts (Brazil nuts are a great choice)

Directions:
1. Preheat the oven to 375°F (190°C) and prepare a casserole dish by greasing it. Put the chicken pieces into the dish and bake for around 30 minutes, or until fully cooked.

2. Fill a large saucepan with water and place it over medium heat. Once boiling, add the parsnips and cook the parsnips for around 15 minutes, or until tender. Remove the parsnips and reserve.

3. Add more water to the now-empty pan and bring to the boil again. Add the beans and blanch for around a minute.

4. In a skillet, heat the olive oil and then add the onions. Sauté until soft and then add the mushrooms, shallots, salt and pepper. Cook until the mushrooms brown and shallots soften. Then add the garlic and sauté for a further minute.

5. Once the onion mixture and parsnips are finished, place all the parsnips, half of the mushroom mixture, and the stock into a blender. Process until smooth.

6. Once the chicken pieces are cooked and out of the oven, add the green beans and remaining half of the mushroom mixture to the casserole dish. Combine well.

7. Top the chicken mix with the parsnip puree. Then sprinkle over the chopped nuts and bake for about 30 minutes.

Freeze it: Allow the casserole to cool completely. Transfer it to the freezer bag or container of your choice. Make sure you label it with the date and dish name.

Reheat it: Thaw in the refrigerator all day. Then transfer into a baking dish, cover with foil and reheat in the oven at 375°F (190°C) for about 25 minutes. You can also reheat portions in the microwave.

Nutrition Facts per Serving:
Calories: 290
Fat: 18 grams
Sodium: 990 mg
Sugar: 6 grams

Protein: 9 grams

Grilled Cilantro Lime Chicken
Serves 4

Ingredients:
1 pound chicken breasts
2 tablespoons grape seed oil
Juice of 2 medium limes
2 garlic cloves (minced)
Handful fresh cilantro/coriander (chopped)
1/4 teaspoon salt
Pinch red pepper flakes

To serve:
1 cup chopped bell peppers
1 cup cherry tomatoes

Directions:
1. In a mixing bowl, combine the oil, garlic, lime juice, cilantro, salt, and pepper.

2. Add the chicken into freezer bags and pour the marinade mix over them.

3. Freeze raw.

Freeze it: Make sure you label it with the date and dish name.

Cook it: Thaw in the refrigerator. Heat the grill or grill pan to medium-high heat, Grill each chicken piece for about 6 minutes per side. The internal temperature needs to reach 165°F (75°C). While grilling, roughly chop the bell peppers and mix with whole cherry tomatoes to make a rustic salad.

Nutrition Facts per Serving:
Calories: 204
Fat: 6.3 grams
Sodium: 329 mg
Sugar: 2.6 grams
Protein: 36.1 grams

Spicy Chicken Burger Patties
Serves 4

Ingredients:
1 1/2 cups ground chicken
1 red bell pepper (finely chopped)
2 green onions (finely chopped)
1 jalapeno pepper (finely chopped)
1/2 cup bread crumbs
1/4 cup fresh parsley (finely chopped)
1 egg
1/2 teaspoon salt

To serve:
Hamburger buns
Salad of your choice (e.g. Roasted bell peppers, sliced tomatoes, mixed greens)

Directions:
1. In a large mixing bowl, beat the egg and then stir in the bread crumbs, salt, and pepper.

2. Mix in the remaining patty ingredients. Use your hands to combine the ingredients well until uniformly distributed.

3. Divide the meat mixture into patties. How big is a matter of personal preference, but remember that larger patties take longer to freeze, thaw, and cook.

Freeze it: Place the uncooked patties into a freezer bag or storage container of your choice. Make sure you label with the date and dish name.

Reheat it: Thaw in the refrigerator.

Cook it: Preheat the outdoor grill, or preheat a non-stick pan to medium-high heat. Lower the heat to medium and place the patties on the grill or in the pan. Grill for about 5 minutes per side, or until the patties are cooked through. Again, if you have a thermometer, the internal temperature should reach at least 165°F (75°C).

Serve warm on a bun and garnished with roasted bell peppers, tomatoes, and mixed greens, or any other garnish or your choice.

Nutrition Facts per Serving (excluding the bun and garnish):

Calories: 188
Fat: 6.6 grams
Sodium: 366 mg
Sugar: 6.4 grams
Protein: 19.3 grams

Chicken Pot Pie Casserole
Serves 4

Ingredients:
1 pound chicken thighs (boneless and skinless)
4 tablespoons olive oil
2 cups chicken stock
2 cups sliced button mushrooms
1 yellow onion (diced)
2 medium carrots (finely diced)
2 garlic cloves (minced)
1/2 teaspoon salt
1/2 teaspoon ground pepper
1/2 teaspoon thyme (fresh or dried)
1 cup peas (frozen are fine)
1 teaspoon Dijon mustard
1 teaspoon fresh lemon juice
1/2 cup flour

For the topping:
6 medium potatoes (peeled and cut into 1/2 inch chunks)
1/2 cup milk
1/4 cup Parmesan (shredded)
2 tablespoons butter
Pinch of salt and pepper

Directions:
1. Bring a large pot of salted water to a boil. Add in the potatoes and boil them until soft. Drain and return them to the pot.

2. Mix the cheese, butter, milk, salt, and pepper into the potatoes and roughly smash them. The mix should still be chunky and have some texture. Reserve and let it cool.

3. Cut the chicken into bite-sized pieces and fry in a skillet on medium heat with the olive oil until browned and cooked through.

4. Add the onions, carrots, and mushrooms to the skillet and sauté until softened. Then add the garlic and sauté for a further minute.

5. Add the flour to the skillet and lightly fry for around a minute. Then add the stock and stir over low heat until it thickens and is lump-free.

6. Let the mixture in the skillet cool.

7. Once cooled, stir the peas, lemon juice, thyme, and mustard into the chicken mixture.

8. Make sure both the chicken and potato mixtures have cooled before assembling and freezing the dish.

Freeze it: Now divide the chicken mixture into four foil dishes (or containers of your choice) and then top each with the smashed potatoes. Cover the dishes and freeze.

Serve it: Thaw in the refrigerator. Heat the oven to 400°F (205°C) and place the dishes on a baking sheet. Bake covered for about 20 minutes, then uncovered for about 5 minutes to brown the tops.

Nutrition Facts per Serving:
Calories: 637
Fat: 20 grams
Sodium: 900 mg
Sugar: 9 grams
Protein: 42 grams

Zingy Ginger Chicken
Serves 4

Ingredients:
1 pound chicken thighs (skinless and boneless, cut into bite-sized pieces)
2 tablespoons grape seed oil
1 red onion (finely sliced)
2 tablespoons ginger (minced)
2 cloves garlic (minced)
2 tablespoons tamari or soy sauce
2 tablespoons raw honey
1/2 teaspoon Chinese 5 spice

To serve:
4 cups spinach leaves

Directions:
1. Heat the oil in a large skillet over medium-high heat and fry the chicken pieces until browned and cooked through.

2. Add the onion and sauté until soft. Then add the garlic and ginger and sauté for a further minute.

3. Turn off the heat and stir through the soy sauce and Chinese 5 spice.

Freeze it: Allow the chicken to cool completely. Transfer it to the freezer bag or container of your choice. Make sure you label it with the date and dish name.

Reheat it: Thaw in the refrigerator. Then reheat the contents in a skillet, oven, or microwave. Add the spinach leaves at the last minute and allow to wilt.

Nutrition Facts per Serving:
Calories: 551
Fat: 24.2 grams
Sodium: 361 mg
Sugar: 3.3 grams
Protein: 68.5 grams

Steamed Chicken Wontons

Serves 4

Ingredients:
10-15 square wonton wrappers (3 1/2 inch)
Flour to dust

Filling:
1 pound ground chicken
2 teaspoons ginger (minced)
3 cloves garlic (minced)
4-5 green onions (sliced)
2 tablespoons tamari or soy sauce
1 teaspoon sesame oil
1 egg (whisked)
3 cups of cabbage (finely shredded)

Directions:
1. In a mixing bowl, combine all the filling ingredients.

2. Lay the wonton wrappers on a piece of parchment paper. Spoon about a tablespoon of the filling onto each one.

3. Fold the wrapper in half over the chicken filling and fold the edges to seal. It should be in the shape of a triangle.

4. Sprinkle flour over the dumplings to stop them sticking.

5. Freeze the chicken wontons raw.

Freeze it: Freeze the wontons on a tray lined with parchment paper for an hour, then transfer them to the freezer bag or container of your choice. Make sure you label it with the date and dish name.

Cook it: Do not thaw the dumplings – they are best cooked from frozen. Using a large pan with a bamboo steamer or metal vegetable steamer (or even your rice cooker) steam the dumplings for about 10 minutes or until cooked through. If you prefer, these wonton dumplings can also be shallow or deep fried from frozen; they take around 5 minutes to cook.

Serve with soy sauce, hot sauce, or any other dipping sauce of your choice.

Nutrition Facts per Serving:
Calories: 480
Fat: 15.2 grams
Sodium: 610 mg
Sugar: 4 grams
Protein: 31 grams

Honey Sesame Chicken Drumsticks

Serves 4

Ingredients:

8 chicken drumsticks
1/2 cup rice vinegar
5 tablespoons honey
1/3 cup tamari or soy sauce
1 teaspoon sesame oil
2 tablespoons grape seed or vegetable oil
1 teaspoon Chinese 5 spice
Pinch ground red pepper
3 cloves garlic (minced)
1/4 cup sesame seeds

Directions:

1. Mix together all the ingredients except for the chicken.

2. Pour the marinade into a plastic bag or storage container and add the chicken drumsticks.

3. Leave to marinate for an hour in the fridge.

4. Preheat the oven to 425°F (220°C).

5. Put the marinated chicken drumsticks into a baking dish and pour over all remaining marinade.

6. Bake for 30 minutes, then baste with the marinade, sprinkle the sesame seeds over the chicken and bake for a further 15 minutes.

7. Make sure the drumsticks are cooked through (the internal temperature should reach reaches 165°F or 75°C).

Freeze it: Allow the chicken to cool, then transfer to the freezer bag or container of your choice. Make sure you label it with the date and dish name.

Reheat it: Thaw in the refrigerator. Then reheat in the microwave or oven until heated through.

Nutrition Facts per Serving:
Calories: 458
Fat: 26 grams
Sodium: 1343 mg
Sugar: 21.3 grams
Protein: 33.5 grams

Pork

Sweet Corn and Ham Mini Quiches
Makes around 24 mini quiches

Ingredients:
6 eggs
1 can sweet corn
1/2 cup all-purpose flour
4 slices ham (chopped)
1/2 cup shredded cheddar cheese
1/2 cup milk
2 tablespoons fresh chives (chopped)
1 teaspoon freshly cracked black pepper

Directions:
1. Preheat the oven to 375°F (190°C) and grease a muffin tin.

2. In a large bowl, whisk the eggs, milk, flour, chives, and pepper together.

3. Then stir through the corn, chopped ham, and shredded cheese.

4. Pour the mixture into the muffin tin, filling each cup about 3/4 of the way.

5. Bake for about 15 minutes, or until golden brown on top. Remove them from the pan and let the mini quiches cool completely. If you're like me, you'll probably snack on a couple at this point!

Freeze it: Freeze on a baking sheet for around an hour, then transfer them to the freezer bag or container of your choice. Make sure you label them with the date and dish name.

Reheat it: Reheat the quiches from frozen. Preheat the oven to 375°F (190°C) and bake for 5-10 minutes.

These mini quiches make a great appetizer, snack, or breakfast. They can also be served with salad and bread for a meal.

Nutrition Facts per Quiche:
Calories: 66
Fat: 2 grams
Sodium: 116 mg
Sugar: 0.7 grams
Protein: 3.9 grams

Sticky Roast BBQ Pork Ribs
Serves 4

Ingredients:
2 pounds pork ribs (country style)
1 cup tomato paste
2 cloves garlic (minced)
1/2 cup malt vinegar
5 tablespoons honey
2 tablespoons Worcestershire sauce
1 teaspoon allspice
1 tablespoon vegetable oil

Directions:
1. Mix together all the marinade ingredients.

2. Place the ribs into a baking dish and pour the marinade over the top. Cover the dish with foil.

3. Roast for 2 hours at 325°F (160°C), then remove the foil and roast for a further half hour. Be careful they don't dry out – if they do, brush with 2 tablespoons of water mixed with a tablespoon of honey.

Freeze it: Let the ribs cool. Transfer them to the freezer bag or container of your choice. Make sure you label them with the date and dish name.

Reheat it: Thaw in the refrigerator. Then reheat in the microwave for about 3 minutes per serving. You can also wrap them in foil and reheat in the oven for about 15 minutes at 350°F (175°C), or until warmed through.

Note: These ribs are also great made in a slow cooker – cook on low for 7 hours.

Nutrition Facts per Serving:
Calories: 505
Fat: 24 grams
Sodium: 524 mg
Sugar: 22.2 grams
Protein: 40.3 grams

Glazed Orange-Apricot Pork Chops

Serves 6

Ingredients:
6 pork chops
3/4 cup apricot jam
1 teaspoon salt
1/2 teaspoon pepper
1/2 teaspoon ground cinnamon
1/4 teaspoon ground ginger
1/4 teaspoon ground cloves
2 mandarin oranges with juice

Directions:
1. Place your pork chops into a roasting tray.

2. Mix the apricot jam with the spices in a small mixing bowl, then pour over the pork chops.

3. Place the mandarin oranges on top.

4. Cover with foil and roast in the oven for around 40 minutes at 350°F (175°C).

Freeze it: Once cooled, transfer the pork to the freezer bag or container of your choice. Make sure you label it with the date and dish name.

Reheat it: Thaw in the refrigerator. Then reheat in the microwave for about 3 minutes per serving. You can also wrap them in foil and reheat in the oven for about 15 minutes at 350°F (175°C), or until warmed through.

Nutrition Facts per Serving:
Calories: 306
Fat: 21 grams
Sodium: 468 mg
Sugar: 17.8 grams
Protein: 18.7 grams

Pork Chops with Creamy Cabbage

Serves 4

Ingredients:
4 pork chops (about 5 ounces meat each)
2 large potatoes (sliced)
1 large yellow onion (sliced)
Drizzle olive oil

For the cabbage:
4 cups green cabbage (coarsely sliced)
1 tablespoon butter
3 tablespoons cream
1/2 teaspoon fennel seeds
Salt and pepper to taste

Directions:
1. Preheat the oven to 350° (175°C).

2. Grease a casserole dish with olive oil, then line it with a layer of sliced potatoes, then a layer of onions. Repeat until all have been used. Depending on the size of your dish, you might only have one layer, or you may have more.

3. Place the pork chops on top and drizzle a little olive oil over them. Roast at 350°F (175°C) for about 40 to 45 minutes, or until cooked through.

4. Meanwhile, melt the butter in a pan over medium heat. Sauté the cabbage until it softens, then remove from the heat and stir through the cream and fennel seeds. Season to taste.

Freeze it: Allow all components to fully cool. Divide the pork, veggies, and cabbage into
four individual portion foil dishes (or containers of your choice). Make sure you label them with the date and dish name.

Reheat it: Thaw in the refrigerator. Then reheat in the oven for about 15 minutes at 350°F (175°C), or until warmed through.

Nutrition Facts per Serving:
Calories: 297
Fat: 27 grams
Sodium: 145 mg
Sugar: 4.3 grams
Protein: 29.3 grams

Apple Cherry Pork Rib Roast
Serves 4-6

Ingredients:
Pork rib roast – aim for around 3 pounds
1 cup fresh or frozen cherries (pitted)
1 cup apples (peeled and diced – Granny Smith are great)
3/4 cup apple juice
1/2 cup water
1 onion (diced)
1/2 cup celery (finely diced)
Salt and pepper to taste

Directions:
1. Preheat your oven to 350°F (175°C).

2. Place the pork into a roasting pan.

3. Combine the remaining ingredients in a mixing bowl and then pour over the pork.

4. Cover with foil and cook for around 1 1/2 hours, or until cooked through (the center temperature should reach 145°F (63°C).

Freeze it: Let the pork cool, then transfer it to the freezer bag or container of your choice. Make sure you label it with the date and dish name.

Reheat it: Thaw in the refrigerator. Then reheat in the microwave for about 3 minutes per serving. You can also wrap it in foil and reheat in the oven for about 15 minutes at 350°F (175°C), or until warmed through.

Nutrition Facts per Serving:
Calories: 261
Fat: 5.4 grams
Sodium: 96 mg
Sugar: 5.8 grams
Protein: 40.1 grams

Mexican Spiced Ham
Serves 4

Ingredients:
1 pound boneless ham
2 tablespoons vegetable oil
1 yellow onion (sliced)
2 cloves garlic (minced)
1/4 cup brown sugar
1/2 teaspoon cayenne pepper
1/2 teaspoon red pepper flakes
1 teaspoon cumin
1 teaspoon paprika
Juice 1/2 lemon

Directions:
1. Combine all ingredients except for the ham in a mixing bowl.

2. Place the ham into a baking dish and rub the marinade mixture into the ham. Roast for 20 minutes at 350°F (175°C). As the ham is precooked, you don't need to worry about it cooking through.

Freeze it: Allow the dish to cool, then slice thinly and transfer to the freezer bag or container of your choice. Make sure you label it with the date and dish name.

Reheat it: Thaw in the refrigerator. Then reheat in the microwave until heated through.

This ham is delicious served with a side salad, with boiled potatoes, or even in soft corn tortillas with your favorite toppings.

Nutrition Facts per Serving:
Calories: 278
Fat: 14 grams
Sodium: 1379 mg
Sugar: 13.76 grams
Protein: 21.8 grams

Beef

Mini Meatloaves
Serves 6

Ingredients:
2 tablespoons olive oil
1 cup carrots (chopped)
1 cup celery (chopped)
1 onion (chopped)
1/2 cup zucchini (chopped)
1/2 cup red bell pepper (chopped)
1/2 cup tomato paste
2 cloves garlic (minced)
2 eggs (lightly beaten)
2 tablespoons balsamic vinegar
2 teaspoons dried thyme
1/4 teaspoon salt
1/4 teaspoon pepper
3/4 cup almond meal
2 pounds ground beef

For the glaze:
2 tablespoons balsamic vinegar
1 tablespoon Dijon mustard

Directions:
1. Preheat the oven to 375°F (190°C) and grease muffin tins (you can make 18 smaller loaves or 12 medium ones, so make sure you have adequate tins).

2. Heat 2 tablespoons of olive oil in a large saucepan over medium heat. Add in the onions and sauté until soft.

3. Next, add in the chopped vegetables and sauté until soft and lightly browned.

4. Add the minced garlic and sauté for another minute. Remove the sautéed vegetable mixture and let it cool.

5. In a small bowl, whisk the eggs, tomato paste, balsamic vinegar, thyme, salt, pepper, and almond meal.

6. Once well combined, mix the beef in.

7. Once the vegetables have cooled, add them into the mixture.

8. Form 18 muffin-sized balls and place them into the prepared tin cups.

9. Mix the glaze ingredients together and brush over the tops of the muffins.

10. Place the tin into the oven and bake for 20 to 30 minutes.

Freeze it: Allow the mini meatloaves to cool completely. Then transfer them to the freezer bag or container of your choice. Make sure you label with the date and dish name.

Reheat it: Thaw in the refrigerator. Then reheat them in the microwave for about 2 minute each.

Nutrition Facts per Serving:
Calories: 486
Fat: 26.6 grams

Sodium: 305 mg
Sugar: 9.2 grams
Protein: 53.6 grams

Mongolian Beef
Serves 8

This is another great recipe to make in bulk in a slow cooker and then freeze the leftovers. We often make this on weekends when we're at home but too busy with other things to dedicate time to cooking.

Of course, you can also make this dish without a slow cooker – simply fry off the beef first and set aside, then add the onions, garlic, and ginger to your pan and sauté, then add all the other ingredients (including the beef) and simmer for around 15 minutes.

Ingredients:
3 pounds beef flank steak (diced)
4 tablespoons vegetable oil
2 teaspoons ginger (minced)
4 garlic cloves (minced)
1/2 cup soy sauce
1 1/2 cups water
3/4 cup honey
2 tablespoons corn starch (or enough to coat the beef)
1 cup carrots (chopped)
5 green onions (chopped)

Reserve:
1 head broccoli florets

Directions:
  1. Start by sprinkling the steak strips with corn starch.

2. Add the remaining ingredients together in the slow cooker and stir to combine well.

3. Add the flank steak to the slow cooker, cover, and let the mixture cook on high for about 2 to 3 hours. Add the broccoli florets and cook for a further half hour.

Freeze it: Allow the contents to cool. Then transfer them to the freezer bag or container of your choice. Make sure you label it with the date and dish name.

Reheat it: Thaw in the refrigerator. Then reheat on the stove top in a stock pot over medium heat until thoroughly heated. Alternatively, reheat in the microwave for around 3 minutes per serve.

***Nutrition Facts per Serving*:**
Calories: 482
Fat: 17.7 grams
Sodium: 965 mg
Sugar: 23.1 grams
Protein: 49.3 grams

Dijon Skillet Feast

Serves 4

Ingredients:

1 pound lean ground beef
2 tablespoons olive oil
1 cup mushrooms (coarsely chopped)
2 medium zucchinis (trimmed and sliced into half-moon pieces)
1/2 teaspoon pepper
1/2 teaspoon garlic powder
1/2 teaspoon salt
1/2 teaspoon dried basil
1/2 teaspoon dried oregano
2 tablespoons Dijon mustard

Directions:

1. Heat a tablespoon of olive oil in a large skillet over medium-high heat. Add in the mushrooms and sauté them for about 4 minutes, or until browned.

2. Add the zucchini, salt, and pepper. Sauté for about 4 minutes or until just tender. Remove from the pan and reserve.

3. Now, add another tablespoon of olive oil to the pan and brown the ground beef. Break up the meat as you brown it. If your pan is small, you may need to brown the meat in batches to avoid overcrowding the pan – remember that you want the meat to brown, not to boil in its own juices.

4. Once the meat is cooked through, mix the veggies back in and add the spices.

5. Lastly, add in the Dijon mustard and mix through.

Freeze it: Let it cool then transfer to the freezer bag or container of your choice. Make sure you label it with the date and dish name.

Reheat it: Thaw in the refrigerator. Then reheat in the microwave for about 3 minutes per serving. You can also wrap in foil and reheat in the oven for about 15 minutes at 350°F (175°C), or until warmed through.

This Dijon skillet beef is really versatile – you can serve it with potatoes, rice, or even pasta. A healthy option is to put it in lettuce leaves and wrap up into tasty bundles.

Nutrition Facts per Serving:
Calories: 237
Fat: 4.3 grams
Sodium: 457 mg
Sugar: 2.8 grams
Protein: 33.8 grams

Succulent Spare Ribs

Serves 6

Ingredients:
4 pounds beef spare ribs
2 cups onions (diced)
2 cloves garlic (minced)
1 cup beef broth
2/3 cup tomato sauce
3 tablespoons soy sauce
2 tablespoons Worcestershire sauce
4 tablespoons honey
2 sprigs fresh thyme
1 teaspoon paprika
1 teaspoon black pepper
2 tablespoons vegetable oil

Directions:
1. Preheat the oven to 350°F (175°C).

2. Season the spare ribs with salt and pepper.

3. Heat a large pan over medium-high heat, heat the oil, and add in the ribs. Brown them on all sides.

4. Next, remove the beef from the pan and set it aside in a baking dish.

5. In a mixing bowl, combine all the other ingredients. Pour the sauce over the ribs in the baking dish and cover with foil.

6. Bake for about 2 hours.

Freeze it: Allow the ribs to cool. Then transfer them to the freezer bag or container of your choice. Make sure you label it with the date and dish name.

Reheat it: Thaw in the refrigerator. Then reheat in the oven, wrapped in foil, for around 15 minutes, or until warmed through.

Nutrition Facts per Serving:
Calories: 478
Fat: 16 grams
Sodium: 627 mg
Sugar: 7.2 grams
Protein: 70 grams

Oregano and Basil Meatballs
Serves 4-6

Ingredients:
1 1/2 pounds ground beef
2 eggs
1 medium onion (diced)
1/2 cup carrots (shredded)
4 garlic cloves (minced)
1 teaspoon oregano (dried)
2 teaspoons basil (dried)
1 teaspoon salt
1/4 cup bread crumbs
2 cups diced tomatoes
1/2 cup water
2 tablespoons tomato paste
1 teaspoon paprika
1/2 cup fresh basil leaves (chopped)
1 tablespoon olive oil

Directions:
1. Pre-heat the oven to 350°F (175°C) and prepare a baking sheet.

2. Combine half the onion with the salt, eggs, carrots, breadcrumbs, dried basil, and oregano in a mixing bowl.

3. Once those are combined, mix in the ground beef.

4. Roll the mixture into 1/4-cup sized balls and line them up on a baking sheet.

5. Bake them for 20 minutes.

6. Meanwhile, place a pan on medium heat and add the olive oil. Sauté the other half of the onion until soft, then add the garlic and sauté for a further 30 seconds. Add the tomato paste and paprika and fry off for around a minute.

7. Add the diced tomatoes and water and let the sauce simmer for around 15 minutes.

8. Let the meatballs and sauce cool completely before combining together, and add in the fresh basil.

Freeze it: Transfer to the freezer bag or container of your choice. Make sure you label it with the date and dish name.

Reheat it: Thaw in the refrigerator. Then heat them in the microwave at 50% power for 2 minutes per 4 meatballs. Serve with freshly cooked pasta – angel hair pasta is a great choice if you're in a rush.

Nutrition Facts per Serving:
Calories: 424
Fat: 13.3 grams
Sodium: 787 mg
Sugar: 9.4 grams
Protein: 58 grams

Lamb

Lamb, Quinoa, and Butternut Squash Pilaf
Serves 6

Ingredients:
1 pound ground lamb
1 pound butternut squash or pumpkin (in small cubes)
1 cup green beans (chopped)
1 yellow onion (diced)
2 cloves garlic (minced)
2 cups quinoa
4 cups vegetable broth
3 tablespoons olive oil
1 teaspoon ground cumin
1 teaspoon ground cilantro/coriander
1/2 teaspoon ground cinnamon
1/2 teaspoon salt

Directions:
1. Heat half the olive oil in a heavy-bottomed pan and fry off the ground lamb until caramelized well. It's important to fry the mince rather than stew it so the flavor enhances. For this reason, you'll need to fry the ground lamb in batches, so you don't overcrowd your pan. Once cooked, put the lamb aside.

2. Next, sauté the diced onion until translucent. Then add the garlic and sauté for a further 30 seconds. Add the ground cumin, cilantro, and cinnamon and fry for around 10 seconds to enhance the flavor.

3. Add the quinoa, salt, and broth to the pan, along with the diced squash and reserved lamb. Cover the pan and cook over low heat for about 15 minutes, then add the beans and cook for a further 5 minutes. When it's ready, the squash should be cooked through and the quinoa should be tender. It's fine if the beans are still crunchy as they will finish cooking when the dish is reheated.

Freeze it: Allow the dish to cool down. Then transfer to the freezer bag or container of your choice. Make sure you label it with the date and dish name.

Reheat it: Thaw in the refrigerator. Then reheat in the microwave for about 3 minutes per serving. Optional – mix through a handful of baby spinach leaves before reheating.

Note: this recipe can be easily converted into a delicious vegetarian treat by simply replacing the lamb with mushrooms.

Nutrition Facts per Serving:
Calories: 473
Fat: 21 grams
Sodium: 513.5 mg
Sugar: 5.3 grams
Protein: 21.7 grams

Comforting Lamb and Vegetable Casserole

Serves 6-8

Ingredients:
1 1/2 pounds stewing lamb meat (cut into chunks)
3 cups potatoes (cubed)
2 cups carrots
1 large onion (diced)
2 cloves garlic (minced)
3 tablespoons olive oil
3 cups broth (lamb or vegetable)
2 cups water
16-ounce can tomatoes (diced with juice, around 2 cups)
1/4 teaspoon celery salt
1 teaspoon rosemary (dried or fresh)
2 teaspoons dried parsley
1 tablespoon Worcestershire sauce

Directions:
1. Place a large pan on medium heat and add 2 tablespoons of olive oil. Add the lamb chunks and brown them. Remove the lamb from the pan and reserve.

2. Add another tablespoon of olive oil to the pan, along with the carrots and onion and sauté until the onion is transparent. Then add the garlic and sauté for a further 30 seconds.

3. Add the remaining ingredients, put the lid on the pan, and leave the casserole to simmer for around 2 hours over medium-low heat.

4. Once cooked, the meat and vegetables should break apart easily and the sauce should have reduced; at this point, adjust the seasoning with salt and pepper to taste. If the sauce reduces too much at any time during the cooking process, simply add a little water.

Freeze it: Allow the dish to cool down in the refrigerator. Then transfer to the freezer bag or container of your choice. Make sure you label it with the date and dish name.

Reheat it: Thaw the bag out in the refrigerator. Then microwave for 2-3 minutes per serve or re-heat on the stove. It can also be reheated in the oven at 325°F (160°C) for about 15 minutes until warmed through.

Note: This casserole can also be made in the oven. Use a casserole dish with a lid and cook at 350°F (180°C) for around 2 hours.

Nutrition Facts per Serving:
Calories: 383
Fat: 9.8 grams
Sodium: 570 mg
Sugar: 6 grams
Protein: 41 grams

Slow-Cooked Lamb Burritos
Serves 8

I like to put this on before I go to work in the morning, then come home to a delicious meal with enough left over to freeze and feed the family another day!

Ingredients:
3 pounds lamb meat (roughly cubed)
6 cups tomatoes (diced – or 3 cans tomatoes)
3 cups red bell pepper (sliced)
3 cups green bell pepper (sliced)
2 red onions (sliced)
8 tablespoons tomato puree
1/2 cup jalapeno peppers (sliced)
4 cloves garlic (minced)
2 tablespoons paprika
2 tablespoons dried oregano
2 tablespoons ground cumin
2 tablespoons ground cilantro/coriander
4 tablespoons vegetable oil

Flour tortillas (for serving)

Directions:
1. In a mixing bowl, combine the paprika, garlic, oregano, cilantro, cumin, and oil and rub the mixture into the meat.

2. Next, place the onion, peppers, tomato puree, tomatoes, and jalapeno into a slow cooker. Mix to combine.

3. Place the meat on top of the vegetables, cover, and cook for 8 hours on low heat.

4. The meat will be very tender. Remove it from the slow cooker, shred it using 2 forks, and then mix it with the sauce and vegetables on the bottom.

Freeze it: Allow to cool. Then transfer to the freezer bag or container of your choice. Make sure you label it with the date and dish name.

Reheat it: Thaw in the refrigerator. Reheat on the stove top over medium heat in a large stockpot, or in the microwave until heated through. Serve with tortillas and fresh salad leaves of your choice.

Nutrition Facts per Serving:
Calories: 255
Fat: 9.7 grams
Sodium: 257 mg
Sugar: 9.9 grams
Protein: 6.3 grams

Lamb and Veggie Shish Kebabs
Serves 4

Ingredients:
1 pound lamb (sliced into 2" chunks)
1 tablespoon olive oil
1 teaspoon garlic powder
1/2 teaspoon oregano
1 tablespoon Worcestershire sauce
Salt and black pepper to taste

To assemble:
1 small onion (cut into large chunks)
2 tomatoes (cut into large chunks – or use whole cherry tomatoes)
2 zucchinis (cut into large chunks)
Bamboo skewers (pre-soak in water, if possible)

Directions:
Mix the seasonings together and rub into the meat.

Freeze it: Place the meat into freezer bags, remove the air, and freeze flat.
Make sure you label it with the date and dish name.

Cook it:
1. Thaw the kebab meat in the fridge during the day.

2. When you get home, preheat your grill to high and cut your vegetables.

1. Thread the meat and vegetables onto the skewers, alternating each ingredient.

2. Grill over high heat, browning them on all sides, until cooked through.

Note: The vegetables are added later to avoid loss of quality. If you choose to freeze your kebabs already on the bamboo skewers together with vegetables, use onion and bell pepper as they perform better.

***Nutrition Facts per Serving*:**
Calories: 336
Fat: 20.3 grams
Sodium: 111 mg
Sugar: 3.3 grams
Protein: 29.3 grams

Lamb Stew with Dried Plums
Serves 4-6

Ingredients:
2 1/2 pounds boneless stewing lamb (chopped into 1" cubes)
3 tablespoons vegetable oil
1 yellow onion (diced)
2 cups carrots (diced)
3 garlic cloves (minced)
1 tablespoon ginger (minced)
1/2 teaspoon cayenne pepper
1/4 teaspoon ground cardamom
1/4 teaspoon ground cinnamon
1 teaspoon salt
Zest of 1 small lemon
2 cups stock (lamb or vegetable)
1 cup dried plums/prunes (pitted)

Directions:
1. Mix the dry spices together and rub into the lamb.

2. Heat 2 tablespoons of oil in a pan over medium high heat, and brown the lamb. Once browned, remove and reserve. Avoid overcrowding your pan – if you need to, brown the lamb in batches.

3. Add the remaining tablespoon on vegetable oil to the pan along with the onion and carrot. Sauté until the onions soften. Then add the minced garlic and ginger and sauté for a further 30 seconds.

4. Return the lamb to the pan and mix in the lemon zest and stock.

5. Bring the contents to a boil, then reduce the heat to low. Cover and simmer for about 2 hours, stirring occasionally.

6. Add in the dried plums during the last 30 minutes of cooking.

7. Once cooked, adjust the seasoning to taste.

Freeze it: Allow the contents to cool completely. Then transfer them to the freezer bag or container of your choice. Make sure you label it with the date and dish name.

Reheat it: Thaw in the refrigerator. Reheat thoroughly on the stove top in a large stockpot over medium heat, or in the microwave, if you prefer.

Nutrition Facts per Serving:
Calories: 427
Fat: 16.2 grams
Sodium: 482 mg
Sugar: 8.3 grams
Protein: 63.6 grams

Vegetarian

Sweet Potato and Black Bean Tacos
Serves 4

Ingredients:
1 1/2 cups cooked black beans (or 16-oz can, drained)
3 cups sweet potato (peeled and cubed)
1/4 cup onion (diced)
2 cloves garlic (minced)
1/2 teaspoon ground cumin
1/2 teaspoon ground cilantro/coriander
1 teaspoon chili flakes
2 tablespoons vegetable oil
1 tablespoon honey
Salt to taste

To serve:
8 flour tortillas
1 avocado (diced)
1/2 cup cabbage (finely shredded)

Directions:
1. Place the cubed sweet potato into a microwave-safe dish and microwave on high for approximately 6 to 7 minutes, or until tender.

2. Heat the vegetable oil in a skillet and sauté the onion until it softens. Then add the garlic and sauté for a further 30 seconds. Add the dried cumin, cilantro and chili pepper and cook for another 10-20 seconds.

83

3. Combine the contents of the skillet with the cooked sweet potato, black beans, and honey. Adjust the seasoning to taste (if using canned beans, you will need very little or no salt).

Freeze it: Allow the dish to cool. Then transfer to the freezer bag or container of your choice. Make sure you label it with the date and dish name.

Reheat it: Thaw in the refrigerator. Then reheat in the microwave for 2 to 3 minutes. Serve the mixture in tortillas, topped with cabbage and guacamole, or any other fresh salad ingredients you have on hand – baby spinach, fresh cilantro, sprouts, grated carrot, and lettuce leaves are also delicious options. You may also like to sprinkle a little shredded cheese on top.

Nutrition Facts per Serving
(including tortillas, avocado, and cabbage)
Calories: 492
Fat: 10.4 grams
Sodium: 405 mg
Sugar: 21.3 grams
Protein: 13.7 grams

Veggie Korma

Serves 6-8

Ingredients:
1 medium head cauliflower (cut into florets)
1 medium eggplant (diced)
1 cup peas (frozen is fine)
2 large potatoes (diced small)
3 tablespoon vegetable oil (don't use olive oil as it's too strong for this recipe)
1 can coconut milk (14 fluid ounces)
1 cup water
1 yellow onion (diced)
2 cloves garlic (minced)
1/2 teaspoon ginger (minced)
1 teaspoon ground cumin
1 teaspoon ground cilantro/coriander
1/2 teaspoon garam masala
1/2 teaspoon ground chili pepper
Salt to taste

Directions:
1. Heat a large heavy-bottom pan, add the oil, and sauté the onion until it softens.

2. Next, add the diced eggplant and sauté for 3-4 minutes until it browns.

3. Add the garlic and ginger to the pan and sauté for a further 30 seconds, then add all the spices and fry for another 10 seconds to release the flavors. Make sure you stir constantly to prevent burning.

4. Place the remaining ingredients into the pan – except for the peas – put the lid on, and simmer on medium-low heat for around 20 minutes. At this point, all the veggies should be tender and the sauce should have reduced slightly. Lastly, add the peas and simmer for a further 5 minutes.

Freeze it: Allow the dish to cool. Then, transfer to the freezer bag or container of your choice. Make sure you label it with the date and dish name.

Reheat it: Thaw in the refrigerator. Then, reheat in the microwave for 2 to 3 minutes. Serve with rice, chapatti, or other flatbread.

Note: You can substitute in other veggies you have on hand as this recipe is really versatile. Some options that work great include: carrots, green beans, mushrooms, and spinach. It's a good idea to have at least one starchy veggie like sweet potato or potato, or even a can of garbanzo beans works well.

Nutrition Facts per Serving:
Calories: 324
Fat: 19.6 grams
Sodium: 57.2 mg
Sugar: 8.7 grams
Protein: 6.4 grams

Spicy Roasted Poblano and Pumpkin Chili

Serves 4

Ingredients:

3 jalapenos (skin and seeds removed, diced)
2 Poblano chilies (skin and seeds removed, diced)
3 medium carrots (diced)
3 celery stalks (diced)
1 yellow onion (diced)
3 cloves garlic (minced)
1 tablespoon vegetable oil
1/2 cup vegetable stock
14-oz. can fire-roasted tomatoes (diced – around 1 3/4 cups)
1 cup pumpkin (pureed)
1 tablespoon ground cumin
1 tablespoon paprika
1/2 tablespoon ground cilantro/coriander
Salt to taste

Directions:

1. Start by roasting the peppers over medium-high heat until the skins are blackened. Place the peppers in a small bowl and cover them with plastic wrap for about 10 to 15 minutes – you want them to sweat.

2. Peel off the blackened skin, remove the seeds, and dice the peppers.

3. Heat the oil in a large stock pot, then add the celery, carrots, and onions and sauté until the onions soften. Then add the garlic and sauté for a further 30 seconds.

Finally, add the dry spices and fry for a further 10 seconds to release the flavors.

4. Add the vegetable stock and tomatoes and cook over medium heat for 10 minutes. The vegetables should be tender.

5. Remove from the heat, add in the pumpkin puree and peppers, and stir to combine. Season to taste.

Freeze it: Allow the dish to cool. Then transfer to the freezer bag or container of your choice. Make sure you label it with the date and dish name.

Reheat it: Thaw in the refrigerator. Then reheat in the microwave for around 3 minutes per serve, or on the stove top until heated through.

Nutrition Facts per Serving:
Calories: 174
Fat: 4.3 grams
Sodium: 218 mg
Sugar: 5.9 grams
Protein: 5.3 grams

Delectable Spinach and Ricotta Balls
Serves 4-6 as a main

Ingredients:
2 1/2 cups frozen spinach
2 cups crackers (crushed)
1 cup Mozzarella cheese (shredded)
1/2 cup ricotta cheese
2 eggs (beaten)
1 tablespoon olive oil
Pinch nutmeg
Freshly ground black pepper to taste
Sea salt to taste

Directions:
1. Thaw the spinach, then squeeze out the excess liquid and discard it.

2. Combine all the ingredients in a mixing bowl.

3. Form the mixture into tablespoon-sized balls.

Freeze it: Place the spinach and ricotta balls on a baking sheet, cover with plastic wrap, and freeze for 2 hours. When completely frozen, remove the wrap and transfer to the freezer bag or storage container of your choice. Make sure you label it with the date and dish name.

Cook it: These spinach and ricotta balls are best cooked from frozen. Preheat your oven to 350°F (175°C). Place the balls on a baking sheet and bake for 20 to 25 minutes, or until golden brown.

...ve as an appetizer, entrée, or side dish, or with rice and salad as a main.

Nutrition Facts per Serving:
Calories: 316
Fat: 12 grams
Sodium: 558.6 mg
Sugar: 0.9 grams
Protein: 16.9 grams

Basic Pizza Dough
Serves 4

Ingredients:
3 cups flour (preferably bread flour)
1 sachet instant yeast (3/4 ounce)
1 cup tepid water
1 tablespoon sugar
1 teaspoon salt
4 tablespoons olive oil

Directions:
1. Put the tepid water into a bowl and stir in the sugar until it dissolves. Then add the yeast and stir until dissolved. Set aside for 5-10 minutes for the yeast to activate.

2. Put the flour into a large bowl, along with the salt. Mix well.

3. Once the yeast mixture is frothy and has activated, add to the flour mixture and combine, along with the olive oil.

4. Once combined into a dough, lightly flour your bench and knead the dough. Do this by folding the dough in half, pressing it out, and repeating.

5. Once the dough becomes elastic in texture, place the it back into the bowl and cover with plastic wrap. Leave the dough in a warm (90-100°F), draft-free place to proof – this will take about half an hour. A good place is the microwave (turned off!).

6. Once it's risen to around double the size, roll out the dough into a rough circle. Remember, it'll still taste delicious even if it's not a perfect circle!

Freeze it: Freeze the raw, rolled-out dough between sheets of parchment paper. Alternatively, you can freeze pizza dough in balls, then defrost in the fridge, roll out, top with your favorite ingredients, and bake.

Cook it: If you have frozen your pizza base already rolled out, cook for 10 minutes at 350°F (175°C), then remove from the oven and add your toppings, and bake for a further 15 to 20 minutes at 450°F (230°C).

I like to make large batches of pizza bases all at once and leave them in the freezer for when we want a family treat. Then we just quickly throw on whatever toppings we have around and can enjoy a delicious, homemade treat.

Nutrition Facts per Serving:
Calories: 301
Fat: 8.9 grams
Sodium: 98 mg
Sugar: 1 gram
Protein: 8 grams

Cheesy Potato and Rosemary Pizza
Serves 4

Ingredients:
1 pizza base (see previous recipe)
1 cup potatoes (sliced and cooked)
1/2 onion (sliced)
2 tablespoons olive oil
2 garlic cloves (minced)
1 cup mozzarella cheese (shredded)
1/4 cups green bell pepper (sliced)
1/4 cups red bell pepper (sliced)
Sprig of fresh rosemary

Directions:
1. Pre-heat the oven to 450°F (230°C).

2. Place the pizza dough on a baking sheet lined with parchment paper (this makes it easier to remove once cooked).

3. Sprinkle the potatoes, garlic, olive oil, and fresh rosemary leaves on the base. Top with the cheese, onion, and peppers.

4. Bake for 15 to 20 minutes, or until the cheese is melted and bubbly.

Freeze it: Allow the pizza to cool. Wrap it firmly, place in a gallon freezer bag and freeze. Make sure you label it with the date.

Reheat it: Do not thaw, bake from frozen on the center oven rack. Heat the oven to 350°F (175°C) and bake for about 20 to 25 minutes.

Nutrition Facts per Serving:
Calories: 554
Fat: 18.4 grams
Sodium: 873 mg
Sugar: 4.8 grams
Protein: 18.7 grams

Desserts

Apple and Raisin Crumble
Serves 6-8

Ingredients:
2 pounds apples (peeled, cored and chopped – Pink Lady and
Granny Smith are great choices)
1/2 cup water
1/4 cup raisins
1/4 cup sugar
1 teaspoon ground cinnamon

For the topping:
1 1/2 cups old-fashioned rolled oats
1/2 cup all-purpose flour
1/2 stick unsalted butter, at room temperature (4 tablespoons)

Foil pans (1 large, 2 medium, or 4 small, depending on the size
of your family).

Directions:
1. Put the apples, water, raisins, sugar, and cinnamon into a
   pan and simmer for around 5 to 10 minutes, or until soft.
   Let the mixture cool.

2. Meanwhile, rub the butter into the flour with your
   fingertips.

3. Then mix the rolled oats into the flour mixture.

4. Place the cooled apple mixture into the foil pan(s).

5. Top with the crumble mixture.

Freeze it: Cover the foil tins and freeze uncooked. Don't forget to label with the dish name and date.

Cook it: Cook the crumble from frozen. Heat the oven to 350°F (175°C) and place the dishes on a baking sheet. Bake covered for around 20 minutes for a small crumble, 30 minutes for medium size, or 40 minutes for a large crumble. Bake uncovered for the last 5-10 minutes to brown the top.

Nutrition Facts per Serving:
Calories: 196
Fat: 6.1 grams
Sodium: 64 mg
Sugar: 24.9 grams
Protein: 3.6 grams

Nutty Freezer Fudge
Serves 8

Ingredients:
1 cup peanut butter
1/3 cup coconut oil
1/4 cup cocoa powder
1/4 cup pure maple syrup
1/2 teaspoon fine sea salt
1 teaspoon vanilla extract

Directions:
1. Mix the peanut butter and coconut oil together until smooth (you can also use a food processor).

2. Add in the cocoa powder, maple syrup, sea salt, and vanilla. Stir until smooth and creamy.

3. Transfer the mixture to a tray and smooth the top with a spatula.

4. Place the tray in the freezer and let the fudge set for about 1 hour before slicing and serving.

Freeze it: Store the leftovers in a sealed container in the freezer.

Serve it: Thaw to desired temperature.

Nutrition Facts per Serving:
Calories: 147
Fat: 12.2 grams
Sodium: 59 mg
Sugar: 3.9 grams

Protein: 3.1 grams

Gluten-Free Almond Cookies

Makes around 2 dozen cookies

Ingredients:
2 cups sifted almond flour
1/2 teaspoon baking soda
1/4 teaspoon salt
3/4 cup chocolate chips
1/4 cup walnuts (roughly chopped)
1/4 cup honey
1/4 cup softened unsalted butter + extra for greasing pan
2 eggs
1/2 teaspoon vanilla extract

Directions:
1. Mix the salt, baking soda, nuts, chocolate, and almond flour together well.

2. In another smaller mixing bowl, melt the honey and mix with the softened butter

3. Add the honey mixture, egg, and vanilla into the flour mixture. Mix it well.

4. Chill the dough in the refrigerator for about 30 minutes.

5. Form into cookie-sized balls.

Freeze it: Place the cookie balls on a baking sheet, cover with plastic wrap, and freeze for 2 hours. When completely frozen, remove the wrap and transfer to the freezer bag or storage container of your choice. Make sure you label it with the date and dish name.

Cook it: Preheat the oven to 350°F (175°C). Line up the dough balls on a baking sheet. Bake for 15-20 minutes, or until the cookies turn golden brown.

Nutrition Facts per Serving:
Calories: 176
Fat: 5.2 grams
Sodium: 17.6 mg
Sugar: 6.2 grams
Protein: 5.1 grams

Strawberries and Cream Popsicles

Makes 12 small popsicles

Ingredients:
3 cups strawberries
1 can full fat coconut milk
1/2 tablespoon vanilla extract
3 tablespoons honey

You will need a Popsicle mold for this recipe.

Directions:
1. Put the strawberries and 1 tablespoon of honey into a food processor or blender and pulse a few times so that the strawberries are partially broken down.

2. In another bowl, mix the coconut milk, vanilla, and 2 tablespoons of honey.

3. Pour 1 to 2 tablespoons of the strawberry mixture into each mold, then 1 to 2 tablespoons of the coconut mix. Switch back and forth until the molds are full.

Freeze it: Allow the popsicles about 6 hours to fully freeze.

Serve it: When ready to enjoy these, you can run the bottom of the Popsicle molds under warm water to help release them from the molds. Serve and enjoy!

Nutrition Facts per Serving:
Calories: 60
Fat: 4.7 grams
Sodium: 3.2 mg

Sugar: 6.8 grams
Protein: 0.7 grams

Mosaic Fruit Popsicles
Makes 12

This recipe is perfect when you have a lot of fruit that's ripened all at once. We love making these popsicles with mango and kiwi, but any fruit works well, with the exception of melons.

Ingredients:
4 cups mixed, diced fruit
1 cup apple juice

You will need a Popsicle mold for this recipe.

Directions:
1. Simply fill each mold with mixed, chopped fruit and then pour over the apple juice.

2. Make sure there are no air bubbles by tapping the molds against the bench.

3. If you make these popsicles using a lot of citrusy or tart fruit, you might like to mix in a couple of tablespoons of honey as well.

Freeze it: Allow the popsicles about 6 hours to fully freeze.

Serve it: When ready to enjoy these, you can run the bottom of the Popsicle molds under warm water to help release them from the molds. Serve and enjoy!

Nutrition Facts per Serving
The nutrition facts will depend on the fruit used. When made with kiwi, mango, and berries, each Popsicle has:

Calories: 35
Fat: 0.2 grams
Sodium: 1.2 mg
Sugar: 6 grams
Protein: 0.4 grams

Paleo Banana Bread
Serves 12

Ingredients:
3 bananas, mashed (about 1 1/2 cups)
3 eggs
1 tablespoon vanilla extract
1 tablespoon honey
1/4 cup coconut oil
2 cups almond flour
1/2 teaspoon sea salt
1 teaspoon baking soda

Directions:
1. Preheat the oven to 350°F (175°C).

2. Combine the bananas, eggs, vanilla, honey, and coconut oil in a food processor. Pulse until the consistency becomes smooth.

3. Next, add in the flour, salt, and baking soda. Pulse until they are mixed in well.

4. Scoop the batter into a greased 7.5" x 3.5" loaf pan and place it into the oven. Bake at 350°F for about 60 minutes.

5. Remove the pan from the oven and let it cool completely.

Freeze it: Slice the bread as desired and transfer to a freezer-safe bag or other storage container. Label and freeze.

Reheat it: Thaw it for a few hours at room temperature, or defrost an individual piece in the microwave for 20 to 45 seconds.

***Nutrition Facts per Serving*:**
Calories: 343
Fat: 11.1 grams
Sodium: 122mg
Sugar: 6.4 grams
Protein: 10 grams

Chocolate Coconut Bark
Serves 8

Ingredients:
1/4 cup dark chocolate
1 cup coconut oil
1 handful coconut flakes
1 handful slivered almonds
1/2 teaspoon sea salt

Directions:
1. Prepare an 8 x 8 inch pan by lining it with parchment paper.

2. Make a double boiler by filling a pot with water, then place a smaller pot on top so it just hovers above the water.

3. Bring the water to a simmer. Break the chocolate into small pieces and melt them in the top pot.

4. Remove the pot with the chocolate from the heat and stir in the coconut oil until melted.

5. Add in the coconut flakes and slivered almonds.

6. Pour the mix into the pan lined with parchment paper.

7. Sprinkle the sea salt on top.

8. Place the dish into the freezer for about 15 minutes until it becomes solid, then break it into pieces.

Freeze it: Store the chocolate coconut bark pieces in a sealable freezer bag or container of your choice.

Serve it: Thaw for a few minutes at room temperature and serve crunchy.

Nutrition Facts per Serving:
Calories: 272
Fat: 29.3 grams
Sodium: 122 mg
Sugar: 3.5 grams
Protein: 0.5 grams

Conclusion

Nowadays, it seems everyone is crunched for time and on a tight budget, but you won't have to sacrifice delicious and nutritious meals ever again! Now that you're armed with the 45 freezer meal recipes in this book, you'll enjoy healthy and tasty homemade cooking without slaving in the kitchen for hours at dinner time. The benefits are many, from the smiles on your family's faces, to the extra time you will have, to the extra money in your pocket, to the relief of stress-free dinner times. All this will make you glad you gave freezer meals a try.

So, what are you waiting for? Time to get cooking!

Printed in Great Britain
by Amazon.co.uk, Ltd.,
Marston Gate.